1. Do you have money saved? Why do you th[ink it is]
important to save your money? Explain.

_____

_____

_____

MW00896677

Cool Money Fact:

2. The largest bill ever printed in the United States was the $100,000 bill, but it was only used for transactions between Federal Reserve Banks.

What would you do with $100,000? Would you spend it all? What would you buy? Would you save some of it?

_____

_____

_____

_____

_____

_____

3. The average American has about $17,000 saved in an emergency fund. Why do you think it is important to have an emergency fund? What expenses should you have enough to cover? Explain your reasoning.

_____

_____

_____

4. The infographic shows a framework of how a budget might be developed. What is one expense that is not included in this graphic? Explain why it would be needed.

_____

_____

_____

_____

_____

_____

5. In 2022 the front of the U.S. Quarter was redesigned. What differences do you notice between the old quarter(left) versus the new quarter(right)? What is written on the quarters?

_____

_____

_____

6. Each one-dollar bill has a unique serial number in green on the upper right hand side of the Washington, usually consisting of two letters followed by eight numbers. The number makes it more difficult for counterfeiters to make fake bills and helps the government to track the movement of money.

What is the serial number on this dollar bill?_____

In what other ways do you think the dollar bill makes it difficult for people from making fake money?

_____

_____

7. For everyday transactions and general use, the highest U.S. bill that most people commonly encounter is the $100 bill. The $100 bill features a portrait of Benjamin Franklin and is widely used for transactions, including purchases, payments, and withdrawals from ATMs.

Who is the man on the $100 bill? Was he a U.S. president? Make 2 other observations about the $100 bill.

_____

_____

8. Throughout history, various forms of money have been used, ranging from shells and beads to precious metals like gold and silver. Over time, societies developed coins and paper currency as standardized forms of money, leading to the diverse currencies we use today.

Why do you think that people used things like shells and beads as money a long time ago? What do you think made people decide what to use as payment?

_____

_____

9. A budget is like a plan for your money. It helps you decide how much to save, how much to spend, and on what things. It's like making a list to make sure you use your money in the best way for you.

Describe a budget in your own words. If you were given $100, how would you budget it? How much would you save, how much would you spend and what would you spend it on?

_____

_____

_____

10. Do you know where the term "buck" came from when referring to U.S. bills? The term originated in the 18th century when deerskin was a common medium of exchange for goods/services.

Summarize in one to two sentences where the term "buck" came from.

_____

_____

11. Budgets should be made with the idea that they can be changed and adapted at any time. What might cause someone to have to adjust their budget? When looking at a long term budget, what might change as a person gets older that they may have to budget for that they never thought of before? Explain.

_____

12. When creating a budget for yourself or your family, every expense needs to be taken into account. Often times pet owners forget to include the cost of having a pet into their yearly budget.
On average, a pet owning household spends about $1,400 a year on their pets.

Is it a good idea to evaluate your budget before getting a new pet? If you have ever got a pet, did you research how much it might cost before getting it?

_____

_____

13. A common budgeting concept is the idea of "pay yourself first". This is the idea that when you get paid you first set aside a portion (anywhere from 2% to 20% or more) of your paycheck for savings before you pay bills or make other purchases. It is a way to prioritize saving for your future self.

Why do you think the concept of "paying yourself first" is so popular? Is this something you would think about doing when setting up your budget?

_____

_____

_____

14. In 2020 the average person spent $23.87 per month on video games and accessories.

What do you spend the most money on per month?

_____

_____

15. There are two main ways that employers pay their employees: Wage and Salary. Wage employees get paid based on a certain period of time such as hourly or daily. Salary employees get paid a set amount of money that is divided throughout the year such as weekly or biweekly pay checks.

What else do you know about the differences? Is one type of job better than the other do you think? Explain.

_____

_____

16. About 56% of people ages 18-24 are currently living with their parents? What are some financial benefits of this choice?

_____

_____

_____

_____

_____

Statistic from Next Gen Personal Finance

17. In the United States our currency system is the U.S. Dollar. There are 180 different types of currencies circulating across 195 different countries.

Can you name any other currencies that are used in other countries? List as many as you can.

_____

_____

_____

_____

_____

18. Many people find that budgeting using the envelope method is successful for them. This method requires dividing your available money (usually in the form of cash) into separate envelopes that represent your key spending categories such as groceries, transportation, clothing, entertainment, gifts, etc. Many budgeting apps now have this strategy virtually as well!

Why do you think this a successful budgeting strategy for some people?

_____

_____

 Money Spotlight

Alexander Hamilton

19. Do you think only U.S. Presidents should be represented on our currency or should we update them to include other influential people in our nation's history? Explain.

Alexander Hamilton is one of two people represented on our U.S. Bills that were never presidents. Hamilton was a founding father who served as Secretary of the U.S. Treasury from 1789 to 1795.

_____

_____

20. "Money is only a tool. It will take you wherever you wish, but it will not replace you as the driver."
- Ayn Rand

What do you think this quote means? Explain.

_____

_____

_____

_____

WANT NEED

21. Identifying if something is a need or a want is found to be a successful budgeting strategy. What are three things that can be considered a need? What are 3 wants?

_____

_____

_____

_____

_____

_____

22. Data shows the 98% of people read online reviews before buying a new product. Is this something you do? Why would looking at reviews be a good consumer decision? Explain.

★★★★★

_____

_____

_____

_____

_____

Statistic from Next Gen Personal Finance

23. Typically once a month the bank sends a statement that lists what transactions were made in and out of your account. This statement may be mailed or sent electronically.

Why do you think it would be important to check this statement to make sure it is accurate? What could you find by looking at this statement?

_____

_____

_____

_____

_____

24. Minimum wage is like a rule that says everyone who works should get paid at least a certain amount of money. It's there to make sure people are paid fairly for the work they do, kind of like a fair-pay rule. What do you think could happen if there was no minimum wage set by the government?

_____

_____

25. Minimum wage is the minimum amount an employer can legally pay an employee. The federal minimum wage as of 2023 is $7.25 per hour. Many states have higher minimum wages.

Do you know what the minimum wage is in your state? Do you think minimum wage is enough money for people to live off of? Why or why not?

_____

_____

Harriet Tubman

26. During the Obama Administration, it was announced that Harriot Tubman would be replacing Andrew Jackson on the $20 bill. This redesign is still in the works but is said to happen by 2036.
Do you know anything about Harriot Tubman? If so, what? Are there any other aspects of our nation's currency you think should be changed?

_____

_____

_____

27. A credit card is a tool that lets you buy goods without carrying cash. It's like borrowing money, but you have to pay it back by the due date or you have to pay extra money to the credit card company, called "interest".

Why do people have to be careful using credit?

_____

_____

_____

_____

_____

28. The first credit card was introduced in 1950 by Diners Club, and it was initially made of cardboard.

What do you know about credit cards? Write 3 things about credit cards.

_____

_____

_____

_____

_____

29. In 1909, Abraham Lincoln became the first president featured on our coins in honor of his 100th birthday.

If you could redesign the penny, who would you put on it? Why?

_____

_____

_____

30. Did you know that in 2022 40% of adults carried a credit card balance from month to month?

What are the downsides of carrying a balance on a credit card from month to month? How can you prevent yourself from carrying debt?

_____

_____

_____

_____

_____

§ YourBank

Your Credit Card Account Statement

Statement Period:
From April 01, 2015
To April 30, 2015

● PAYMENT INFORMATION

New Balance:	$ 3663.23
Your Minimum Payment:	$ 36.63
Your Minimum Payment Due Date:	May 24, 2015

Account Number:
9999 99XX XXXX 1234

Primary Cardholder:
Yourname Yoursurname

Estimated time to pay

The estimated time to pay your New Balance in full if you pay only the Minimum Payment each month is 2 year(s) and 4 month(s)

● SUMMARY OF YOUR ACCOUNT

Previous Statement Balance:	$ 2654.48
Payments:	$-2654.48
New Purchases:	$ 1957.24
Balance Transfers and Access Cheques:	$ 1200.00
Cash Advances	$ 500.00
Interest:	$ 0.00
Fees:	$ 5.99
Subtotal	$ 3663.23
Your New Balance:	$ 3663.23
Credit Limit:	$ 9000.00
Cash Advance Limit:	$ 500.00
Credit Available:	$ 5336.77
Cash Advance Limit:	$ 0.00
Statement Closing Date:	April 30, 2015
Days in Statement Period:	30
Annual Interest Rate for Purchases:	19.99%
Annual Interest Rate for Balance Transf. and Access Cheques:	2.50%
Annual Interest Rate for Cash Advances:	19.99%

Ways to Pay:
Online Banking
Telephone Banking
ATM
Pie-Authorized Payment
By Mail To:
YourBank
P.O. Box 1234 Section Z
BankCity, NY, 98456

Contact Information:
www.websitename.com
Customer Service/Lost or Stolen
1-888-123-4567
TTY/TDD
1-888-123-4567

31. The minimum payment on a credit card is the smallest amount of money you have to pay back each month. It's like the least you can do to keep your account in good standing. However, it's usually better to pay more if you can to avoid extra charges and paying a lot of interest.

What is the full balance in this statement? What is the minimum payment? Subtract the balance from the minimum payment, what is the difference?

_____

_____

_____

32. For hundreds of years people have been throwing coins into fountains like the Trevi fountain in Rome. It is said that throwing a coin into a fountain will bring you good luck. Most of the time this money is donated to charity. About $4,000 is collected and donated from the Trevi fountain every day.

Have you ever thrown a coin into a fountain? If so where? Did it bring you good luck?

_____

_____

_____

_____

 _____

_____

33. The image below shows monthly expenses. Fixed expenses are the expenses that occur regularly every month and do not typically change much in cost. What are three examples of expenses that you can expect to pay the same amount at the same time every month?

HOUSING INSURANCE FOOD TRANSPORT **MONTHLY EXPENSES** ENTERTAINMENT CLOTHING INTERNET MOBILE COMMUNICATIONS

_____

_____

_____

_____

FINANCIAL LITERACY BRAIN TEASER

34. Would you rather have $1,000,000 or start with a penny and double your money every day for 30 days? Why?

_____

_____

_____

. When writing a check you need to write both the numeric and the written form of the amount to avoid any discrepancies or misunderstandings about the ayment amount. Practice this by filling in the chart.

Numeric	Written Form
125.65	
	Two thousand six hundred twenty-three dollars
5,678.59	

36. Before electronic banking, checks hysically traveled from the issuing bank to he recipient's bank. This process could take several days. Now banking can happen most immediately because of technology.

How could people benefit from the traveling of checks before electronic banking?

_____

_____

_____

_____

_____

37. The Wall Street Journal says that people make their smartest financial decisions between ages 53-54. What are some factors that might explain this trend?

_____

_____

_____

_____

_____

38. Our U.S. paper currency has 6 key security features to prevent counterfeiting. Can you name three of them?

_____

_____

_____

39. The Federal Trade Commission is the government agency that handles fraud complaints from consumers. In 2021 there were 2.8 million fraud reports. 1 in 5 people lost money and the average loss was $1,000. The most popular scam was an imposter scam where the scammer was pretending to be someone else.

Why do you think there has been an increase in people losing money to these imposter scams?

_____

_____

_____

_____

40. Continuing with the statistic from the #39, what is one warning sign that something could be a scam?

_____

_____

_____

41. In a 2020 study done by Intuit Min 3 out of 5 people had no idea how mu money they spent the month before What are the benefits of knowing ho much you spent in a given month?

_____

_____

_____

_____

American Women Quarters

42. Featured women include: Maya Angelou, Dr. Sally Ride, Anna May Wong, Bessie Coleman, Eleanor Roosevelt, Rev. Dr. Pauli Murray, Celia Cruz, Ida B. Wells, Althea Gibson and many more.

Are there any other notable women or people that should be honored on our currency? Why?

_____

Starting in 2022 a 4-year program was initiated to honor women in our history. Each year 5 new quarters would be released each highlighting a trailblazing American women. "The ethnically, racially, and geographically diverse group of individuals honored through this program reflects a wide range of accomplishments and fields, including suffrage, civil rights, abolition, government, humanities, science, space, and the arts." ~U.S. Mint

Consumers mobile banking app activities, by generation

Generation	Total	Gen Z	Millennials	Gen X	Boomers
View account balances	86.5%	86%	89.5%	86.5%	78%
View account statements	68%	62%	73.5%	67%	61.5%
Transfer money between bank accounts	64%	65.5%	71.5%	60.5%	50%
Deposit checks	59.5%	58%	66%	54%	53.5%
Pay bills	49%	45.5%	53%	50%	40.5%
Check credit score	32%	28.5%	56.5%	30%	20%
Use peer-to-peer payments	24%	20%	31%	21.5%	14.5%
Use online chat to ask a question	16.5%	18%	27.5%	13%	12.5%
Create and track a budget	13.5%	25%	17.5%	9%	4%
View a forecast of monthly spending	13%	17%	18%	9.5%	4.5%
Create a savings goal and track progress	12%	21.5%	18%	5.5%	2%
Open a new bank account	9.5%	11.5%	12%	7%	5.5%

Chart from a 2023 Chase Bank Study

Mobile baking apps are popular among most people. Use this chart to answer the question below.

43. By looking at the chart, what is one trend that surprises you? Why? What is one trend that does not surprise you? Explain.

_____

_____

44. Apps like Venmo, PayPal and Zelle allow users to send money electronically to another person. They allow for instant and convenient transfers from one person to another. Many businesses are even accepting these apps as forms of payment. What is one advantage of using these money transfer apps? One disadvantage? Explain.

_____

_____

_____

45. According to Forbes, 6% of households in the United States are unbanked which means that no one in their household has a bank account. This number has been slowly increasing in recent years.

Why do you think some people prefer not to keep their money in the bank? What is the benefit of having a bank account?

_____

_____

_____

_____

_____

cool money fact:

46. The U.S. Dollar is made of 75% cotton and 25% linen. The paper is made specifically for the Bureau of Engraving and Printing by Crane Currency in Dalton, Massachusetts. It is illegal for anyone else to produce this special paper blend.

What is one question you have about how money is produced?

_____

_____

_____

_____

47. Writing checks may seem outdated for some but many people still use checks to pay their monthly bills. There are times that a check is still the best way to pay someone. What do you know about checks? Does anyone in your house use them? Have you ever recieved one?

_____

_____

1	The date	6	The dollar amount of the check in numbers (ex. $19.65)
2	Your name- sometimes the address and phone number are included	7	The financial institutions (bank) name and phone number
3	Pay to the Orderof line- the person or company you are paying	8	The memo section- this is optional but where you can write the reason you wrote the check
4	The check number- this is used to identify each check written from your checkbook	9	The signature line- this confirms it is you writing the check and that you are agreeing to pay the amount of the check to the payee
5	The dollar amount written out in words (ex. nineteen and 65/100)	10	The routing number and account number that the money is coming from

8. Checks must be signed with our unique signature to certify that it is you that wrote the check. Practice writing your name in cursive on the lines.

_____

_____

_____

49. Using Day 35's diagram as a guide, write this check out to your school for a upcoming school dance. Tickets cost $20.50.

	0001

Date _____ 20 _____

PAY TO THE
ORDER OF _____ $ [_____]

_____ DOLLARS

🔒 Security Features Details on Back

For _____   _____

⑈005552222⑈   ⑈005552222222⑈ 0001

---

50. In order to deposit a check, you must endorse the check on the back by signing your name. Checks can be deposited in person at the bank, through an ATM and now many banks are accepting check deposits through their mobile apps.

What is the benefit of the bank allowing check deposits through the mobile app? Can you think of any negatives of this feature?

_____

_____

51. What would be one benefit of writing a check instead of paying with cash or credit card?

_____

_____

_____

_____

_____

_____

52. When looking at a paystub from a job you are able to see your 'gross pay' and your 'net pay'. Gross pay is what you earned before taxes, benefits and other deductions. Net pay is the amount remaining after all those deductions. It can also be called your 'take-home pay'. Your net pay is the amount that you receive in the form of a check of direct deposit.

Why is it important to know the difference between your gross pay and your take-home pay?

_____

_____

_____

. Federal taxes are collected from any individual or company that earns income. They are based on a percentage of their income. The government uses taxes for things like maintaining roads and airports, supporting scientific research and maintaining natural resources.

What are two other examples of things the federal government might use this tax money for?

_____

_____

_____

Fast Finance Fact:

54. As well as federal taxes, many states have state income tax. Only 7 states do not have state income tax. They pay tax other things but not an individuals or companies income.

Does your state have income tax? Do you know how it compares to other surrounding states?

_____

_____

_____

_____

COMPANY NAME					EARNINGS STATEMENT		
Some Corporation 123 Somewhere Drive, Durham, NC 12345				95220			
EMPLOYEE NAME		SSN	EMPLOYEE ID	CHECK NO.	PAY PERIOD		PAY DATE
Hope Marie Kingsley		xxx-xx-6789	98856	98765	5/1/2018 - 5/15/2018		5/21/2018

INCOME	RATE	HOURS	CURRENT TOTAL	DEDUCTIONS	CURRENT TOTAL	YEAR-TO-DATE
GROSS WAGES	15.00	40	600.00	FICA MED TAX	8.70	78.30
				FICA SS TAX	37.20	334.80
				FED TAX	90.00	810.00
				NC ST TAX	34.50	310.50
				HEALTH	$76.58	$689.22
				DENTAL	$8.23	$74.07
				RETIREMENT*	$60.00	$540.00

YTD GROSS	YTD DEDUCTIONS	YTD NET PAY	CURRENT TOTAL	CURRENT DEDUCTIONS	NET PAY
5,400.00	2,836.89	2,563.11	600.00	315.21	284.79

*Excluded from federal taxable wages

Image from Next Gen Personal Finance

Here is an example of a pay (earnings) statement. Please review it and answer the question below.

55. What is the pay period for this earnings statement? _____

56. Using the example earnings statement above, how much has this person paid this year in Federal Taxes?
Note: YTD= Year to Date

_____

57. Using the example earnings statement above, what is this person's YTD gross earnings?

_____

58. Now that you have had a chance to review an example earnings statement, what are two things that surprised you about this statement? What is one question you still have about how receiving pay from an employer works?

_____

_____

_____

_____

_____

Benjamin Franklin

Describe Benjamin Franklins' accomplishments in 2 sentences.

59. Ben Franklin is one of 2 people featured on our U.S. Bills that were not presidents. He is said to have played a key role in building the U.S. He was the only founding father to have signed the three most important documents that led to Independence: Treaty of Alliance with France, Treaty of Paris and the Declaration of Independence.

_____

_____

60. Mobile payment services such as Apple Pay and Google Pay allow you to make a payment by just holding your phone near a payment terminal. They also add another layer of protection by changing your credit card number to protect your information when giving it to the business.

How do you think Apple Pay and other payment services have changed the way people make payments? Are there any potential concerns about using these mobile payment systems?

_____

_____

_____

_____

61. In 2020 8.9% of people over 75 are still working. This number has been steadily increasing and projected to reach 11.7% by 2030. Why do you think people over 75 are still working? What steps could you take now if you are not interested in working into your 70s?

_____

_____

_____

_____

_____

_____

_____

Statistic from Next Gen Personal Finance

62. Credit cards have 4 pieces of important information on them:
-Cardholders Name
-Card Number
-Expiration Date
-CVC (card verification code)

Do you know how a credit card differs from a debit card? Write two ways they differ below.

_____

_____

_____

_____

63. One new feature coming to many credit cards is the ability to tap to pay. This is a form of RFID or Radio Frequency Identification. The technolog inside the chip of your credit card transmits the information wirelessly to the receivers that are placed inside payment terminals.

Have you ever used a tap to pay credi card? If so, how was that experience? How was it different from other credit card methods such as swiping or inserti the chip?

_____

_____

_____

64. The average credit card interest rate in the U.S. for 2023 is 21.9%. That means if you only pay the minimum balance on your credit card and carry a balance from one month to the next, you are paying 21.9% interest annually.

Why is it important to know the interest rate on your credit card?

_____

_____

_____

_____

65. RBR Global predicts that by 2026 81% of all cards will be contactless. What is one pro and one con of this prediction?

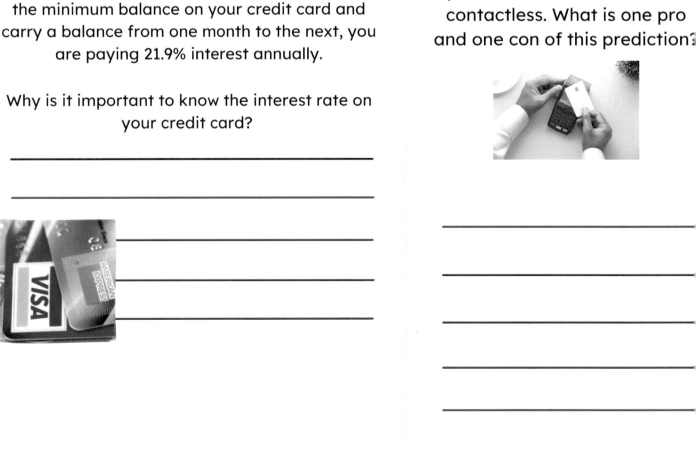

_____

_____

_____

_____

_____

66. Prioritizing your needs over your wants can be helpful when trying to stick to a budget. Circle <u>only the needs</u> from the words below.

utilities	brand new shoes	vacation	groceries
healthcare	Netflix Subscription	insurance	candy
video games	winter coat	basic clothing	transportation
water	ice cream	house	iphone15

67. Variable expenses are the expenses that change from month to month. They change based on the decisions that you make. They can include things like:
-the cost of eating out at restaurants
-a credit card bill
- the cost of personal care

What are three other variable expenses you can think of?

_____

_____

_____

68. Taking time to write down what you have spent money on for the past 30 days is the first step in any budget creation. What category have you and your family spent the most money on in the past 30 days? (i.e. shopping, food, games etc.)

_____

_____

69. The 50/30/20 budgeting method is one of the most popular rules for budgeting. The rule says that 50% of your monthly income should go to needs such as rent, groceries, and utilities. 30% should go towards wants such as subscriptions, going out to eat and new clothes. The last 20% should go towards savings.
This method allows for you to meet your savings goals without giving up the things you want.

What is one thing that might be difficult about this budget plan?

_____

_____

_____

70. If your take home salary was $90,000 answer the following questions about your 50/30/20 budget plan.

How much would you budget for your needs? (50%)

_____

How much would you budget for your wants? (30%)

_____

How much would you budget for your savings? (20%)

_____

_____

71. Using the credit card below, answer the following questions.

What is the card number?

_____

What is the expiration date?

_____

What is the CVC code?

_____

Money Spotlight: Dr. Sally Ride

Dr. Sally Ride is one of 5 women featured in the 2022 American Women's Quarters program. A 4 year program in which each year 5 notable women in U.S. History would be featured on the back of a quarter. Dr. Sally Ride was a physicist, astronaut, educator, and the first American woman to soar into space.

72. If you had to pick another group of people to be featured on our coins for a number of years who would you pick? Explain your choice.

_____

_____

_____

FINANCIAL LITERACY BRAIN TEASER

73. Would you rather get 1 million dollars right now or $100,000 a year for the rest of your life? Why?

_____

_____

_____

_____

_____

_____

_____

74. A credit limit is the total amount you can borrow on any given line of credit such as a credit card. Once you reach that limit, the card may decline.

What could a person do so that they do not have to fear reaching their credit limit?

_____

_____

_____

_____

_____

75. Unit price is the price at which a single quantity of a product is being sold. This can refer to the price per unit of measure, such as the price per pound, ounce, or pint. The unit price is frequently displayed on the shelves in a supermarket to help shoppers compare between different brands or products of different sizes. It allows for shoppers to get the best deal when looking at items. Many times it is easily displayed and other times it is not.

Here is a grocery store label for Gatorade powder. You can see the unit price in the orange box. What does it say the unit price is?

_____

76. The formula for unit price is

$$unit\ price = \frac{price}{size}$$

For example if a 36 pack of fruit snacks costs $5.25 the unit price would be calculated like so:

$$\frac{\$5.25}{36} = \$0.15\ per\ pack$$

A 24 pack of water bottles is $3.25. How much is one water bottle?

_____

77. You want to sell chips at a school basketball game to raise money for your upcoming field trip. If box of chips has 40 bags of individually wrapped chips in it and the whole box costs $8.46 how much would you need to charge for each bag of chips to make your money back. Show your work.

_____

_____

78. Unit price is best used to compare different sizes of the same product. Complete the chart below.

Remember $unit\ price = \dfrac{price}{size}$

Item	Price	Size	Price per Unit
General Mills Cheerios	$4.99	18 ounces	
General Mills Cheerios	$3.29	14 ounces	
Store Brand Toasted Oats	$2.50	14 ounces	

79. What box of cereal from the chart to the left is the best deal? Why?

_____

_____

80. One problem with unit price is there are no regulations on it. Stores can label them however they want. This makes it difficult for consumers to compare unit prices without having to calculate it for themselves while trying to shop. What do you think? Should there be a universal unit price label to help out consumers or not?

_____

_____

_____

_____

81. Taking the time to compare expenses can help you to best organize your budget. The two main types of expenses are fixed expenses and variable expenses. Fixed expenses occur regularly from month to month and do not change much. Variable expenses change from month to month based on the decisions you make.

Statistic from Next Gen Personal Finance

For each of the expenses below, <u>circle</u> whether that is a fixed or a variable expense.

Rent: Fixed or Variable

Cell Phone Bill: Fixed or Variable

Groceries: Fixed or Variable

Personal care items: Fixed or Variable

Utilities: Fixed or Variable

Gifts: Fixed or Variable

Fast Facts

82. It is important to be able to make quick change in your head when working with cash. Try and solve the following problems in your head:

You buy a candy bar that costs $3.25 with a $5 bill. How much change should you get back?	
Your new sweatshirt costs $36.40. You may with 2 $20 bills. How much change should you get back?	
You and your friend go to the movies. Each ticket costs $5.50. You pay for both tickets with $15. How much change should you expect back?	
You went school supply shopping for the new year. Your total was $76.58. You paid with 4$20 bills. How much change should you expect back?	

83. A new car is one of the biggest purchases someone might make in their lifetime. As of 2023, th average price for a new car is $48,808. What advice would you give someone looking to buy a new car when it came to how they should budget for this car?

_____

_____

84. Debit cards & credit cards may look very similar but they are different. They are both forms of payments but a debit card is your own money, coming directly out of your checking account. A credit card is a loan from the bank that you must pay back later. Can you think of when it may be good to have a credit card?

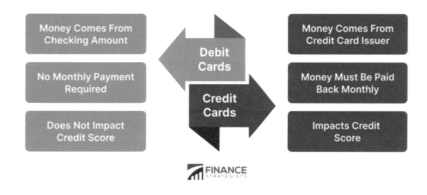

_____

_____

85. A credit card is a loan from the bank that must be paid back later. Credit card companies charge you interest if you do not pay off the whole balance every month. The average annual percentage rate (APR) is 21.9% as of 2023. If you divide the APR (21.9%) by 12 months you will find the monthly periodic rate or what you will be charged the next month on that balance.

If you carry a balance of $2,045 on your credit card, how much interest will you have to pay next month?

_____

$$\frac{APR}{12 months} = \textit{Monthly period rate}$$

Monthly period rate x balance carried = next months interest payment

Show your work:

86. Your friend just opened their first credit card. What advice would you give them before they start making purchases?

_____

_____

_____

_____

_____

87. Credit cards can be convenient for emergencies. Since the money is a loan from the bank, it may be for more than you have at a given time in your checking account. These emergencies could include, your car breaking down and needing to be fixed or a window breaking in your house that needs repair.
What others ways could having access to a credit card be helpful?

_____

_____

_____

88. Mary wanted to buy a new TV for her birthday. She wanted to get it today since it wo on sale. The TV costs $325. When she looked at her checking account, she only have $27 Which form of payment should she use: debit, credit or either? Explain your choice.

_____

_____

89. Mike worked hard and saved up $350 for his new gaming system. The gaming system was on sale so it was only going to cost $275. He wanted to be debt free, so which form of payment should he use: debit, credit or either? Explain your choice.

_____

_____

90. Wage and salary are two common types of pay an employee might get paid. It varies based on the type of job you have and the company you work for. Wage is an amount paid based on a certain time period. You can earn a certain wage per hour, day or week. Some jobs that are paid by wage are many of those in the trades such as electricians, plumbers, factory workers, etc.

Can you think of any other jobs where the employees are commonly paid by wage?

_____

_____

91. Mariam just got a new job at the mall. Her boss told her that she is going to get paid $13.50 per hour. What type of pay is Mariam getting from her new job: wage or salary? Explain your choice.

_____

_____

_____

. There are pros and cons to both wage and salary jobs. A salary type of pay is a fixed amount that you get paid typically for the year. It is then divided and paid out on a weekly or biweekly basis. Salaries can more reliable in the long-term, because they provide a consistent source of income regardless of how many hours worked. Your paycheck tends to be the same amount every week. You may also have more benefits from your employer.

Why might getting paid the same amount every paycheck be helpful when budgeting versus it changing based on how many hours your worked with a wage job?

_____

_____

_____

93. Sam just gradated college and got a job working at a new company. His boss told him her is going to earn $51,300 a year. What type of pay is Sam's new job: wage or salary? Explain your choice.

_____

_____

94. The FDIC or Federal Deposit Insurance Corporation was created by Congress in 1933 to maintain the publics confidence in the nation's financial system. The FDIC insures money in member banks up to $250,000. This means as long as your money is in an FDIC Insured bank, nothing can happen to it if something was to happen to the bank.

Why is it important to check to make sure your bank is insured by the FDIC before you put money into it?

_____

_____

95. You decided to buy new headphones that cost $549 and put the purchase on your credit card. If your credit card has a 24% interest rate and you choose to only pay off the minimum balance each month (4%), it will take you 4 years and 6 months to pay off that credit card. In the end you would pay $324.04 in interest making your headphones cost a total of $874.04.

What does this example show you about only paying the minimum balance on your credit card each month?

_____

_____

_____

Statistic from Next Gen Personal Finance

Cool money fact:

96. Have you ever found a torn bill? U.S. bills are not made to last forever. In fact the U.S. Currency Education Program has found that the average lifespan of a $10 bill, before it is too damaged to continue to be used in circulation, is about 4.5 years. They found that $100 bills have the longest lifespan lasting about 15 years.

Why do you think some bills last longer than others in circulation? Do you know what to do if you have a bill that is torn or ripped?

_____

_____

_____

_____

 97. 28% of individuals age 18-29 have invested in, traded or used cryptocurrency.
What do you know about cryptocurrency? Do you know any of the names of cryptocurrencies?

_____

_____

_____

98. With the increase of online banking and electronic payments, only about 8% of the world's currency is literal cash with the rest of it existing in electronic bank accounts. Do you see any problems with this? Explain your reasoning.

_____

_____

_____

_____

_____

Money Riddle

99. I have a head and a tail but my eyes can never see my tail. What am I?

_____

_____

100. List three reasons why everyone ages 12-18 should take the time to educate themselves about financial literacy.

_____

_____

_____

_____

Financial Literacy Answer Key

1- Answers will vary. Possible answers: to save for things you need.

2- Student answers will vary

3- Answers will vary. Possible answers: you should save enough for food, housing, possibly vehicle, medical expenses, etc.

4- Car insurance, heating, child care, vet visits for pets, etc.

5- Differences- facing different way, different hair style. Written on- Liberty, In God we Trust, the date

6- B 03542754, Possible answers: overlapping text, many items on dollar, woven threads inside the money

7- Benjamin Franklin, he was not president, possible observations: has a serial number, 100 printed 4 times, secretary of treasury signature, United States Federal Reserve symbol, etc.

8- Because they were valuable to the people and they wanted to trade for them.

9- Answers will vary

10- Possible answer- the term buck came from when people in the 1700s exchanged deer skin as currency and male deer are called "bucks"

11- Possible answer- if they buy a house or car, have children, retire, etc.

12- Possible answer- yes, it is a good idea to evaluate a budget before buying a pet because they cost quite a bit of money over time

13- Possible answer- it helps to build savings and investments by paying yourself first. It is a way to stay focused on long-term financial well-being

14- Answers will vary

15- Possible answers- salary is more consistent and if you need to take a day off for illness, you are still paid usually. Hourly may offer more overtime opportunities

16- To save for their future, not have to pay rent, expenses that they may not be able to afford until they have a higher paying job, etc

17- Possible answers:

Eurozone: Euro (EUR)

United Kingdom: British Pound Sterling (GBP)

Japan: Japanese Yen (JPY)

Canada: Canadian Dollar (CAD)

Australia: Australian Dollar (AUD)

Switzerland: Swiss Franc (CHF)

China: Chinese Yuan (CNY)

India: Indian Rupee (INR)

Brazil: Brazilian Real (BRL)

Russia: Russian Ruble (RUB)

South Africa: South African Rand (ZAR)

Mexico: Mexican Peso (MXN)

18- Possible answer- It is a straightforward and easy-to-understand method. This provides a clear visual representation of how much money is allocated to each category, making it easier to track and manage expenses

19- Student answers will vary

20- Possible answers- you can make money but it will not make your life decisions for you, you need to make the right decisions

21- Student answers will vary. Possible answers needs- food and shelter. wants- cell phone, nice clothing, etc.

22- It can give you information on the item you are buying from other consumers so that you can make the right decision

23- It is important to look at statements for mistakes, fraud, overcharges, etc. It also shows you your spending patterns

24- businesses could pay whatever they wanted and possibly abuse workers, there could be more discrimination, etc.

25- Students answers will vary

26- Students answers will vary. Possibly, that she lead many out of slavery during the 1800s. Possibly more women and people of color included on money

27- You will have to pay it back and it may increase due to interest. It could ruin your credit if you don't pay it back in a timely fashion

28- Students answers will vary

29- Students answers will vary

30- If you carry a balance, you are paying more money in the form of interest. Paying your credit card as you spend, is the best way to use them because you won't pay interest

31- Full balance- $3,663.23 minimum payment- $36.63 Difference- $3,626.60

32- Student answers will vary

33- Housing, insurance, internet, mobile communications (cell phone)

34- I would rather start with a penny and double my money every day for 30 days. The power of compounding in this case leads to a significantly larger amount compared to the fixed $1,000,000. It illustrates the concept of exponential growth and the potential benefits of compounding over time

35-

Numeric	Written Form
125.40	one hundred twenty five dollars and forty cents
	Two thousand six hundred twenty three dollars
5,578.59	Five thousand six hundred seventy eight dollars and fifty nine cents

36- They had time to put the money in the bank before someone cashed it

37- They may be nearing the end of their career and thinking about retirement, they are not taking as many risks, etc

38- Security threads and strips, watermarks, color shifting ink, microprinting, holograms, raised printing, etc

39- The rise of internet banking and people hacking others' accounts. Revealing secure information online that may be leaked, etc.

40- Websites you don't recognize, phone calls from out of the state/country, people asking for your information or for money, etc.

41- So that you can budget properly. To know if you are spending too much in one area. To help you set future financial goals, etc

42- Students answers will vary

43- Students answers will vary

44- Advantage- easier and you don't have to go to the actual bank. Downfall- may be harder to tell if it is really someones' check, if the signature is legitimate

45- Possible answers- Some people may have a general distrust of financial institutions. This lack of trust can stem from past negative experiences, concerns about fees, or perceptions of banks as untrustworthy. Some people want to use cash to pay for things to avoid credit problems and bouncing their account. Benefits of banks- many offer interest on your money, helps build credit, easy to pay others securely, etc.

46- Students answers will vary

47- Students answers will vary

48- Students answers will vary

49-

[check image: Lake Shore High School $20.50, Twenty dollars and fifty cents, School Dance]

43- $810, Some Corporation

44- Student answers will vary

45- $5,400

46- Student answers will vary.

47- People don't necessarily need anything but their phone to pay, could leave room for fraud if phone is stolen, possible payment errors, harder to keep track of what you are spending.

48- Possible answers- things are more expensive, people live longer, saving for retirement helps, putting away money so you can retire earlier.

49- You don't necessarily need the money in the account with a credit card, credit cards charge interest.

50- Benefit- you don't need to go to the bank, it is so much easier to deposit through the phone. Possible disadvantage- possible errors due to images, possibly less secure.

51- It may be easier to keep track of the money you spend through your checking account.

52- Because your take home pay is less than your gross pay and you don't want to overspend because you think you have more money coming than you actually do.

53- education, health care, national defense, research, debt payments, etc.

54- Student answers will vary.

55- 5/1/2018- 5/15/2018

56- $810

57- $5,400

58- Student answers will vary.

59- Student answers will vary.

60- People now can pay right from their phones and do not need to carry a credit card or check book if they don't want to. Concerns- possibly less secure, etc.

61- The cost of living has increased, many people live longer due to modern medicine, want nicer trips and items, etc.

62- credit card- you can spend more than you have, affects your credit, may not need pin, etc.

debit card- only allows you to spend what is in your account, does not affect credit, need a pin.

63- Student answers will vary.

64- To understand how much you will be charged if you don't pay in full by due date.

65- Pros- Easy to use- don't have to insert card, less hand contact, less germs Cons- possibly less secure

66-

67- groceries, travel, hobbies, gifts, etc

68- Student answers will vary.

69- This budget can be restrictive and does not take into consideration your values, lifestyle and money goals. For example, 50% for needs is not enough for those in high-cost-of-living areas

70- Needs- 45,000 Wants- $27,000, Savings- $18,000

71- credit card number- 2658 4185 9934 0206

expiration date- 03/20

CCV code- 418

72- Student answers will vary.

73- Student answers will vary.

74- pay off their credit card balance so they still have enough of a limit. Have good credit by paying their bills and credit cards to reach a higher limit

75- $3.47 per pound

76- $0.14

77- about 20 cents (best to sell for $.25)

78-

Item	Price	Size	Price per unit
General Mills Cheerios			
General Mills Cheerios			
Store Brand Toasted Oats			

79- Store brand toasted oats

80- Student answers will vary.

81-

Rent- Fixed or Variable		Coos- Fixed or Variable	
Cost of Groceries- Fixed or Variable		Car Insurance- Fixed or Variable	
Lunches- Fixed or Variable		Gifts- Fixed or Variable	

82-

You buy a candy bar that costs $1.25 with a $5 bill. How much change should you get back?	$3.75
Your new sweatshirt costs $36.40. You pay with 2 $20 bills. How much change should you get back?	$3.60
You and your friend go to the movies. Each ticket costs $5.50. You pay for both tickets with $15. How much change should you expect back?	$4
You went school supply shopping for the new year. Your total was $16.58. You paid with 4 $20 bills. How much change should you expect back?	$3.42

83- Student answers will vary.

84- possible answers- to build credit, to purchase something you need but don't have the cash for.

85- $3,732

86- Possible answers- only spend what you have and pay off the card as quickly as you can so that you don't pay interest.

87- To build credit, to purchase something you need that you don't have the money for right away, to earn points for travel, etc. if you are able to pay the balance.

88- She would have to use credit because she doesn't have enough. It would be better for her to save up and buy the tv when she has the money.

89- He should use debit to be debt free because that is money that he has.

90- Waiters/waitresses, life guard, cleaners, etc.

91- Wage because she is getting paid by the hour.

92- Because salary can be more consistent and you know what you are going to have in the bank for bills and budgeting purposes. Wages may change depending on your availability, the amount of work needed, etc.

93- Salary, it is a set amount for the year.

94- So that if the bank fails or the market crashes, your money is insured.

95- It will cost you much more in the end.

96- They may have been saved or in a bank for a long time. You can tape them and bring them to the bank for an exchange.

97- it is a digital currency, which is an alternative form of payment created using encryption algorithms. Examples: bitcoin, litecoin, dogecoin, stellar

98- Possible answers- If something ever happens to the internet, it could be a problem. No physical exchange, etc.

99- Coin

90- Student answers will vary Possible answers- to prepare themselves for the future, so they are financially stable and do not make large mistakes that will lead to debt, etc.

Made in United States
Troutdale, OR
08/18/2024

22126373R00021

Essential money skills and every 8-12 year old should know! With 100 questions, this workbook makes learning about budgeting, saving, needs vs. wants, credit fun!

Money Spotlight: **Dr. Sally Ride**

Dr. Sally Ride is one of 5 women featured in the 2022 American Women's Quarters program. A 4 year program in which each year 5 notable women in U.S. History would be featured on the back of a quarter. Dr. Sally Ride was a physicist, astronaut, educator, and the first American woman to soar into space

72. If you had to pick another group of people to be featured on our coins for a number of years who would you pick? Explain your choice.

_____
_____
_____

FINANCIAL LITERACY BRAIN TEASER

73. Would you rather get 1 million dollars right now or $100,000 a year for the rest of your life? Why?

_____
_____
_____
_____
_____

74. A credit limit is the total amount you can borrow on any given line of credit such as a credit card. Once you reach that limit, the card may decline.

What could a person do so that they do not have to fear reaching their credit limit?

_____
_____
_____

49. Using Day 35's diagram as a guide, write this check out to your school for an upcoming school dance. Tickets cost $20.50.

```
                                              0001

                          Date _____ 20 ____

PAY TO THE
ORDER OF _____  $ [        ]

_____ DOLLARS

For _____
⑈005552222⑈   ⑈005552222222⑈ 0001
```

50. In order to deposit a check, you must endorse the check on the back by signing your name. Checks can be deposited in person at the bank, through an ATM and now many banks are accepting check deposits through their mobile apps.

What is the benefit of the bank allowing check deposits through the mobile app? Can you think of any negatives of this feature?

51. What would be one benefit of writing a check instead of paying with cash or credit card?

_____
_____
_____
_____

A QUESTION A DAY FOR 100 DAYS!

Twins And Teaching

LPN PM EE286 0269
9 798869 586148

900